Summarizing

Focusing on Main Ideas and Details and Restating in Concise Form

Grades 1-2

by
Renee Cummings

Instructional Fair
An imprint of Carson-Dellosa Publishing LLC
Greensboro, North Carolina

Instructional Fair

Author: Renee Cummings
Editors: Mary Hassinger, Elizabeth Flikkema, Alyson Kieda
Cover Artist: Laura Zarrin

Instructional Fair
An imprint of Carson-Dellosa Publishing LLC
PO Box 35665
Greensboro, NC 27425 USA

ISBN 978-0-74240-105-1
102107784

About the Book

Summarizing involves the skills of comprehending, focusing on important information, and reiterating it in a concise form. *Summarizing 1–2* uses guided activities that help develop and achieve this skill. Students will progress from selecting main ideas and details to writing their own summaries. As this skill is practiced and achieved in reading, the student will naturally begin to use the skill in writing and speaking. Summarization is a concept used throughout the curriculum. Social studies, science, language, and reading all use the skill of summarization in writing, reading, and oral lessons.

This book contains cross-curricular topics as well as fiction. It provides opportunities for students to summarize material that is familiar and relevant to daily life such as maps, lists, recipes, and schedules.

Table of Contents

 Name _____

Pet Shopping

| kite | collar | book | bed |
| leash | fish bowl | dog dish | football |

Use the words above to correctly complete the sentence.

_____

- - - - - - - - - - - - - -

Dusty is our dog. We want to get him a new _____ ,

_____ _____

- - - - - - - - - - - - - - - - - - - - - - - -

_____ , _____ , and

- - - - - - - - - -

_____ . He needs them.

Yard Work

(Look at the pictures and read the words.)

baseball	hoe	mop	wheelbarrow
rake	book	mower	telephone

Use the words above to correctly complete the sentence.

_____

Pam and Dad work in the yard. They use a _____ ,

_____ , _____ , and

_____ . They work very hard.

Fun at the Park

Look at the pictures and read the words.

swings	slide	car	bars
teddy bear	ice skates	merry-go-round	squirrel

Use the words above to correctly complete the sentence.

_____

I went to the park. I played on the _____,

_____ _____

_____ , _____ , and

_____ . I had a lot of fun!

Try This: On the back of this paper, draw and
color a picture of yourself having fun at a park.

It's a Party!

Read the story. Color the pictures
to answer the questions below.

There are balloons.

There is a birthday cake with candles.

There are gifts.

Annika's friends are at her house.

Today Annika is six years old.

1. Who is the story about?

2. What is happening in the story?

Write words from the story to complete the sentences.

_____

Annika is having a _____ party.

_____

She is _____ years old.

Insect Sightings

(Read the sentences and the lists below.)

Maya and Carl went outside to the garden to look for insects. Each of them wrote a list of the insects they saw.

Maya's List		
ants		5
butterflies		2
bees		1
ladybugs		3
grasshoppers		1
flies		0

Carl's List		
ants		4
butterflies		3
bees		2
ladybugs		7
grasshoppers		1
flies		4

Cut out the insect pictures at the bottom of page nine. Paste the correct picture in each box.

1. Maya saw more _____ than anything else.

 Name _____

Insect Sightings (cont.)

2. Carl saw more  than anything else.

3. They both saw the same number of 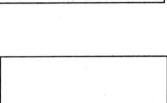 .

4. Altogether, Maya and Carl saw five 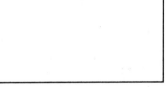 .

5. Carl saw two  .

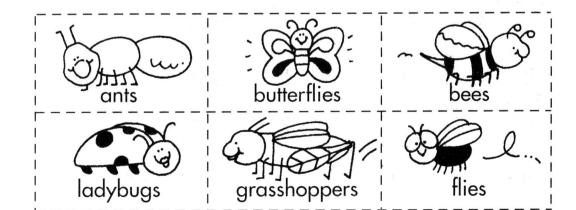

ants   butterflies   bees

ladybugs   grasshoppers   flies

IF5640 Summarizing

A Cool Time

> Read the party invitation. Use it to answer the questions below.

An
Invitation
Just For You

What: A pool party
Given by: Stephen Nguyen
Where: Stephen's house
1234 Coldwater St.
When: Tuesday, July 9
Time: 11:00 A.M.
There will be a picnic lunch
served. Bring your swimsuit
and your swimming fins!

Circle the picture that correctly answers the question.

1. What kind of party is it?

2. Who is giving the party?

3. What foods might be served at the party?

A Cool Time (cont.)

4. What items do you need to bring to the party?

5. What time is the party?

  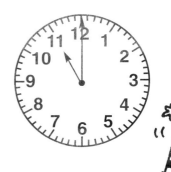

Design your own party invitation.

	What:
	Given by:
	Where:
	When:
	Time:

Making Sense of It

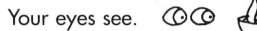
Read the story. Circle the correct answers below.

Clink, clink, clink! Your ears hear.

Your eyes see.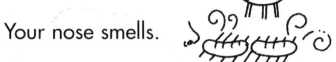

Your nose smells.

Your hands feel.

Your tongue tastes.

Your five senses help you enjoy your world!

1. What would be a good title for this story?

    A Picnic   Hot Dogs   Helpful Senses

2. How many senses do you have?

    three   five   six

3. Which part of your body helps you hear things?

4. Which part of your body helps you smell things?

Name _____

Lucy and Rosita

Read the story below.

Friends are special.
Lucy and Rosita are friends.
They ride the bus to school together.
They go to the circus together.
They help each other read.
They are happy to be together.

Circle the correct answer for each question.

1. What is the story about?

      pets   friends   frogs

2. What word describes friends?

      bus   circus   special

Color the picture that shows friends.

Time for School

Read the story below. Look for details.

Andy is excited! He has a new backpack. It is red and blue. He puts pencils, crayons, a ruler, and a pencil box in his new backpack. Andy is ready for school!

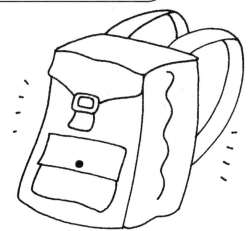

Circle the correct pictures to answer each question.

1. Who is excited?

2. What does Andy have in his backpack?

  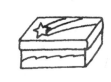

3. What is Andy getting ready for?

Try This: Correctly color Andy's backpack at the top of this page.

Growing

Read the story. Look at the pictures carefully.
Circle the correct answer for each question below.

Josie opened the book. She looked at the pictures. She looked in a
mirror. She was even bigger now than in the pictures. She can do
more things because she is bigger.

1. What is the best title for this story?

    Baby Josie   Josie Grows Up   Funny Pictures

2. What was Josie doing?

    She was looking at pictures of her dog.

    She was looking at pictures of her friend.

    She was looking at pictures of herself.

Write words from the story to complete each sentence.

_____

Josie is _____ now.

Josie can now do _____ things.

Home, Sweet Home

> Read the story. Then circle the word that completes each sentence.
> Write the word on the line.

Every animal has a home. Animals make their homes in different places. Birds build nests in trees or on the ground. Bees build hives in trees or under the ground. Ants and moles build homes under the ground. Bears and bats live in caves.

_____

1. Every animal has a _____ .

   pillow   car   home

2. Some animals build homes in _____ .

   trees   grass   rocks

3. Some animals have homes under the _____ .

   deck   ground   car

4. Other animals have homes in _____ .

   caves   coves   stores

Name _____

School Workers

When summarizing, look for important or key words.

Many people work in a <u>school</u>. <u>Teachers</u> help us learn. <u>Custodians</u> keep our school clean and safe. <u>Bus drivers</u> safely get us to school and back home again. <u>Cooks</u> make meals and help us to grow strong and healthy. People at school really <u>care</u> about us.

Use the underlined words to finish the sentences below.

Many people work in a _____ .

Some of these people are _____ ,

_____   _____

_____ , _____ ,

_____

and _____ .

School workers _____ about us.

Yard Sale

Cut out the categories at the bottom of this page.
Paste the correct category in the box above each list of sale items.

Sam's family is having a yard sale. They made a list of everything they wanted to sell. It was too much to put on a sign. They decided to write only the categories and very short lists on the sign.

Yard Sale

1.

2.

crib
playpen
highchair

Saturday
Only!!!
8:00–5:00

lantern
tent
sleeping bags

3.

4.

bed
sofa
desk

bat
mitt
baseball

Art Supplies   Furniture   Baby Things

Camping Equipment   Pet Things   Baseball Equipment

What a Recipe!

Read this tasty recipe. Circle the correct answers below.

Super Good Chili—Enough to feed six hungry people.

2 pounds (9 kg) ground beef
1 chopped white onion
1 chopped green pepper
2 tablespoons (30 mL) mild chili powder
3 cans dark chili beans
2 cans stewed tomatoes

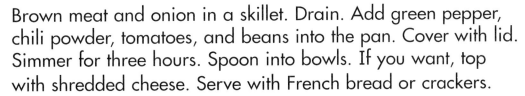

Brown meat and onion in a skillet. Drain. Add green pepper, chili powder, tomatoes, and beans into the pan. Cover with lid. Simmer for three hours. Spoon into bowls. If you want, top with shredded cheese. Serve with French bread or crackers.

1. How many different ingredients are in the recipe?

   2   3   6

2. How many pans must you use?

   1   3   3

3. How long does it take to cook it?

   4 hours   2 hours   3 hours

4. What can you put on top of the chili?

   crackers   cheese   sesame seeds

5. What two things can you serve with the chili?

   rolls   crackers   French bread   breadsticks

6. How many people will you be able to feed?

   four   six   ten

Picture Perfect

Mark is on a trip. Read the postcard he sent to his friend Jeff. In the box below, draw a picture of the place Mark is describing.

Dear Jeff,

We are right here! I swam in this blue lake. My Dad and I hiked that mountain! My Mom took our picture in front of this big tall tree. This place sure is fun!

Your friend,

Mark

Jeff Hillton

1563 Brighten Road

Portville, Oregon 97321

Where's Sassy?

Read the poster carefully. Use the information to circle the correct answers below.

Sassy is missing!

Sassy is an orange, black, and white spotted cat. She has yellow eyes. She has a blue collar with a heart-shaped tag. Please call Shanina at 235–2134 if you see her.
Thank you!

1. What is this?

    a newspaper ad

    a poster

    a book

2. Who has lost something?

    a store

    a dog

    a girl

Use details from the poster to draw and color a picture of what is missing. Write the name of what is missing on the line.

_____

Name _____

The Morning Route

This map shows the route the school bus takes to pick up the children every morning. Circle the correct answer for each question. Use the map to help you.

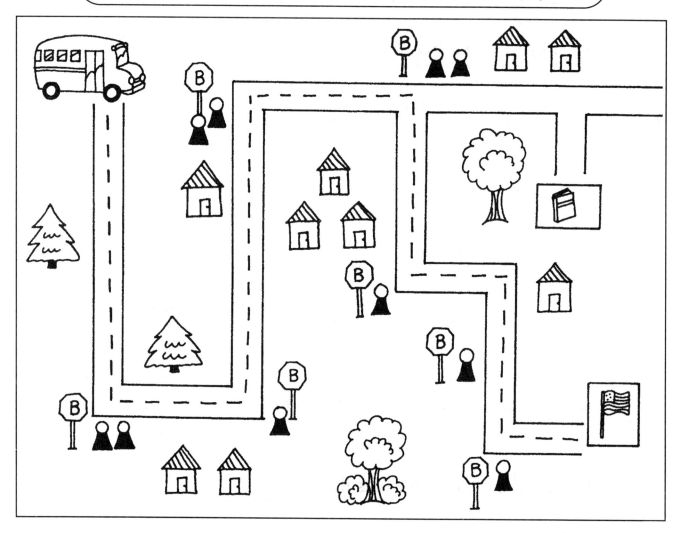

1. What time of day does the bus drive on this route?

    morning   afternoon   night

2. How many stops does the bus make?

    three   five   seven

Key

🛑(B) Bus Stop

👤 Child

🏠 House

🏫 School

📖 Library

--- Bus Route

The Morning Route (cont.)

3. How many children ride the bus?

      seven   nine   ten

4. Where does the bus take the children?

      zoo   school   home

Use the answers you circled to complete these sentences that summarize what is on the map.

In the _____ , the bus stops at

_____ bus stops to pick up _____

children. The bus then takes them to _____ .

Try This: Draw and color a map of your route to school. Include a picture of the vehicle that you ride in on your trip. Show how many people ride in the vehicle with you each day.

Name _____

Watch Out!

Read the story. Circle the correct answer for each question below.

Bertha Butterfly fluttered over a fence. She landed on a flower. She felt movement near her. Bertha looked up just as a kitten's paw reached for the flower. Away she flew! The kitten watched the empty flower move up and down.

1. Who is the story about?

   Belinda Butterfly   Bertha Butterfly   Betsy Bug

2. Where did she land?

   on a fence   in a tree   on a flower

3. What tried to catch her?

   a kitten   a boy   a girl

4. Did it catch her?

   yes   no

Try This: On the back of this paper, draw, and color a picture of what happened in this story.

Name _____

Any Mail Today?

Joey watched the mail truck stop at his house. This is what he found inside the mailbox. Look closely at the illustrations below and answer the questions.

1. Who went to the mailbox? _____

2. How many letters were in the mailbox? _____

3. How many packages? _____

4. How many magazines were in the mailbox? _____

Fill in the blanks to summarize the story. Use the answers from above.

_____ _____ _____

_____ found _____ letters, _____

package, and _____ magazines in the mailbox.

Piñatas

Read about piñatas. Use the paragraph to help complete the activity.

Most festivals in Mexico have a piñata. A piñata is made by gluing strips of paper onto a clay pot or a blown-up balloon. When it dries, it is decorated with brighter, colorful paper. Most piñatas are shaped like animals. Candy and toys are placed inside the piñata.

Match the beginning of each sentence to the correct ending. Write the letter in the blank.

_____ 1. Mexican festivals often have

a. with candy and toys.

_____ 2. A piñata is made

b. of paper, glue, and a pot or balloon.

_____ 3. A piñata is often shaped

c. a piñata.

_____ 4. A piñata is filled

d. like an animal.

Try This: Color the picture of the piñata. Make it colorful!

Maria's Turn

Read about Maria. Draw and color
pictures that summarize the story.

Maria is excited! The donkey-shaped
piñata is hanging from a branch. It is
just above her head. It is Maria's turn.
She puts on the blindfold. She swings
the stick. She swings again. Crack! The
piñata breaks. Candy and toys fall to
the ground. Maria and the other
children quickly pick up the treats.

Tide Pool Peering

Read about Samantha. Then circle the correct words to complete each sentence. Write the words on the lines.

Samantha stared into the tide pool. Tiny fish darted around among the rocks. Two starfish were on the rocks. Four small crabs crawled in the sand. The tide came in and covered the rocky pool. Samantha moved back to the sandy beach.

1. This story is about a girl named _____ .

Suzanne   Samantha   Shania

2. She was looking at a _____ .

beach   lake   tide pool

3. She saw _____ , _____ ,

and _____ .

fish   squid   starfish

sharks   crabs   jellyfish

Look Up!

Read the story. Circle the correct answers below.

It's a helicopter! It flies up and down. It flies forward, backward, and even sideways. It can hover over just one spot. A helicopter is very useful. It can be used to help rescue people and report traffic and news. A helicopter can also lift huge pieces of equipment to the tops of tall buildings.

1. This paragraph is about a ___.

    hummingbird   helicopter   airplane

2. It can fly in ___.

    many directions   one direction   two directions

3. It is __.

    useless   very useful

Use the words you circled to help complete these sentences.

This is a paragraph about a _____. It can fly

in _____ _____ so it is

_____ _____.

A Suitable Name

> Read the story. Write the underlined words on the lines to complete the summary.

Sometimes a <u>lizard</u> is given a <u>name</u> because of the way it <u>looks</u>. A <u>frilled</u> <u>lizard</u> can spread the skin around its neck so it looks like a <u>frilly</u> <u>fan</u>. Specks of blue, red, and yellow make it very colorful.

_____

A _____ can be named for the way it

_____ . The _____

_____ got its _____

because its neck skin can spread out to look like a very

_____ _____

_____ _____ .

> **Try This**: Correctly color the picture of the frilled lizard.

What's a Moropus?

Imagine finding the skeleton of an animal that lived long ago. The animal's bones look like they could be from two different animals! A moropus is an ancient relative of the horse. It had a head and a body like a horse. Its front legs were a little longer than its back legs, and it had feet like the claws of an anteater. These claws were probably used to dig up roots for food.

Draw a picture of a moropus and what it ate.

Petra's Piggy Bank

Petra had been saving money for a long time. She wanted to buy a new kite to fly in the contest on Saturday. The one she wanted looked like a parrot with yellow, blue, green, and red feathers. It costs five dollars. Petra opened her piggy bank and poured her money out on the desk.

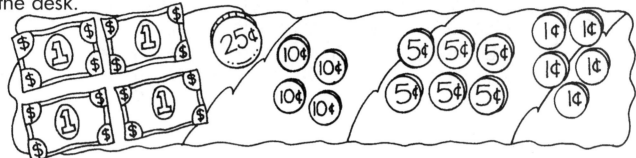

Read the story. Circle the correct answers below.

1. Who is this story about?

   Penny   Petra   Paulo

2. What has she been doing?

   flying kites   saving parrots   saving money

3. Why was she saving money?

   for a contest   to buy a bike   to buy a kite

4. What does the one she wants to buy look like?

   a dragon   a parrot   a pig

5. How much does it cost?

   five dollars   two dollars   four dollars

6. Did she save enough money?

   yes   no

Platypus

Read the story. Circle the correct answers.

The platypus lives in Australia. Its
nickname is "duckbill." It has a snout
that looks like a duck's bill. It has
webbed feet and a flat tail that helps it
to swim. A platypus eats worms and
other small water animals. A platypus is
nocturnal, which means it rests during
the day and hunts for food during the
late evening.

1. Where does a platypus live?

   Australia   Austria   Denver

2. What is the platypus's nickname?

   Donald Duck   duckbill   Dudley

3. What helps the platypus swim?

   webbed feet   snout   soft fur

4. When does a platypus look for food?

   late evening   mid-morning   afternoon

"Bee" Strong

> Read the story. Circle the correct answers below.

Buzz Bee landed beside a piece of cat food. It was much bigger than he. "Hmmmm," he buzzed. He thought he was very strong. Buzz just had to try and lift it! He hovered over the food and grabbed it with all six legs. Buzz flapped his wings. Up he flew! He's strong!

1. Who is this story about?

   Betty Bee   Bob Bobcat   Buzz Bee

2. What did he think he was?

   strong   weak   tired

3. What was he trying to lift?

   crumb   cat food   cookie

4. How big was it compared to him?

   smaller   bigger   same

Use the answers you circled to help you complete the summary. Write the words on the lines.

This is about _____ _____.

He was _____ enough to lift a piece of

_____ _____ that was

_____ than he.

Oops!

Read the story. Use the underlined words to correctly complete the summary.

A little gray <u>mouse</u> scampered up to the glass door. Its tiny black eyes <u>peeked</u> through the <u>glass</u> <u>door</u>. Its pink nose twitched. The <u>cat</u> raised its head and <u>looked</u> out the glass door. This <u>scared</u> the mouse! It turned and <u>raced</u> back to the <u>woodpile</u>. The cat yawned and went back to sleep.

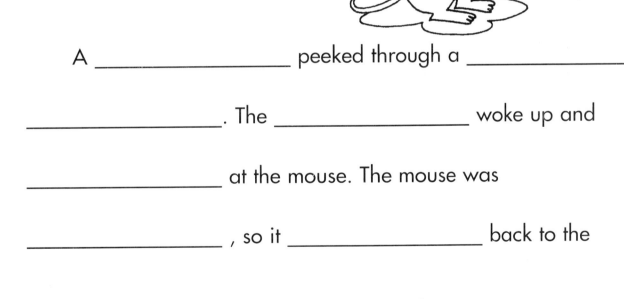

A _____ peeked through a _____

_____ . The _____ woke up and

_____ at the mouse. The mouse was

_____ , so it _____ back to the

_____ .

Try This: On the back of this paper, draw and color a picture of what happened in this story.

Name _____

An Old-Time Train Ride

Read the train schedule. Use it to answer the questions.

Ghost Town Train Ride

Leave **Virginia City**	8:00 A.M.
Arrive **Gold Hill**	9:00 A.M.
Arrive **Genoa**	10:00 A.M.
Arrive **Dayton**	11:00 A.M.
Arrive **Sutton Creek**	12:00 P.M.
Return to **Virginia City**	1:00 P.M.

Adults $15.00

Children $8.00

1. Where does the train ride start? _____

2. What time does the train ride begin? _____

An Old-Time Train Ride (cont.)

3. At how many places does the train stop between leaving and

returning to Virginia City? _____

4. How long is the round-trip train ride? _____

Use your answers to help you write a short advertisement for this

train ride.

_____

_____

_____

_____

_____

_____

Name _____

Pete's Plant

Read the story. Find and circle
the underlined words in the puzzle below.

Pete <u>planted</u> one tiny <u>seed</u>. <u>Every</u> <u>day</u> he <u>watered</u> the seed. One
morning he saw a speck of green. It was a plant! It <u>grew</u> to be three
feet tall. A big bud was at the very top. One morning Pete filled the
watering can and walked outside. Pete was so happy! The tiny seed
was now a big, yellow <u>sunflower</u>!

s	w	a	t	e	r	e	d	n	p	r	t	d	t
e	v	p	g	s	g	m	e	k	g	h	c	r	f
e	v	e	r	i	e	v	e	r	y	l	d	a	y
d	s	t	e	u	r	i	g	a	o	n	j	g	i
o	n	e	w	a	s	u	n	f	l	o	w	e	r
p	l	a	n	t	e	d	b	e	p	l	e	n	i

Use the words you circled in the puzzle to complete the sentences that
summarize the story.

_____ _____ a _____ .

He _____ it _____ _____ .

It _____ into a big, yellow _____ .

Name _____

Just Fold It

Look for key words while reading the story.

Origami is an art in Japan. Many beautiful and useful things can be made by just folding a square sheet of paper. You can make a bird that flaps its wings. You can make a cup for drinking water. You can even make a hat to wear on your head.

Use the key words to complete the summarizing sentences.

Origami is an _____ in _____.

It is the art of _____ a square

_____ of _____. Origami can

be used to make many _____ and

_____ things.

Name _____

Dressed for the Parade

Read the story about Tuffy. Use the story
to fill in the blanks below.

Tuffy is a bulldog. Today Keisha is
dressing him in a costume. She puts a
red and blue striped hat on his head.
Then she snaps a red ruffle around his
neck. She ties a string to his collar. A
yellow balloon bounces above his head
when he walks. They are ready for the
parade.

Keisha is dressing her dog _____ in a

_____. They are going to be in a _____.

Draw and color a picture to show how Tuffy looks in his costume.

What a Change!

Read the story. Use information from
the story for the answers below.

Brad scooped a tadpole out of the
creek. It looked like a tiny fish. It had a
long tail and gills. Brad kept the
tadpole. Its tail grew bigger. It swam
more easily. Then hind legs appeared.
Soon it grew front legs, too. Its head
began to change shape. One day its
gills and tail were gone. It had
grown into a frog!

Write complete sentences to answer the questions.

1. What did Brad scoop out of the creek? _____

_____

2. Name one way the tadpole changed. _____

_____

3. What did the tadpole finally become? _____

_____

Where's Dinner?

> Read about bats and their eating habits. Use the story to answer the questions below. Use complete sentences.

Most bats eat insects. They use their voices and ears to find them. Bats make quick, high-pitched sounds as they fly around. The sounds echo or touch an insect and bounce back to the bat. The echo tells the bat how far away the insect is and where it is moving.

1. What animal is this story about? _____

_____

2. What do many bats eat? _____

_____

3. How do bats find insects? _____

_____

4. What does an echo tell a bat? _____

_____

A Seasonal Thing

Read the essay very carefully. Underline important words and sentences. Use the words and sentences that you underline to write a summary on the lines below.

There are four seasons. They are called winter, spring, summer, and fall. Winter is the coldest season. Summer is the hottest time of year. In spring, it is warm, and plants begin to grow and bloom. Fall is cool, and animals begin to store food. Each season is different.

_____

_____

_____

_____

_____

Name _____

Strong Winds

Read this paragraph. Think about the differences between a hurricane and a tornado. Then describe each one on the lines below.

Wind is moving air. Very strong, fast winds can become hurricanes or tornadoes. A hurricane begins over an ocean. It moves to land. The center or "eye" of a hurricane is calm. The outside is made of whirling, rainy clouds. A tornado is shaped like a funnel. It swirls. It touches the ground. Then the tornado rises and moves across the land. There is often no rain.

Hurricane: _____

_____

_____

Tornado: _____

_____

_____

Shooting Stars

Read this article carefully. Underline key information about meteors. Write a summary below. Be sure to write complete sentences.

Suddenly a light streaks across the night sky. It disappears. It is a meteor. Many people call it a "shooting star." Meteors are rocks that fall into the earth's atmosphere. They come from far out in space. Most meteors burn up before they reach the earth. Mostly meteor dust and very small pieces land on the earth, however some meteors have actually landed on the earth. These are called meteorites.

_____

_____

_____

_____

_____

Answer Key

Pet Shopping 4

collar, bed, leash, dish

Yard Work 5

hoe, wheelbarrow, rake, mower

Fun at the Park 6

swings, slide, bars, merry-go-round

It's a Party! 7

1. girl
2. cake
Sentences: birthday, six

Insect Sightings 8–9

1. picture of ants
2. picture of ladybugs
3. picture of grasshoppers
4. picture of butterflies
5. picture of bees

A Cool Time 10–11

1. boy swimming
2. boy
3. hot dog, hamburger, chips, soda
4. swimsuit, fins
5. clock that reads 11:00
6. Invitations will vary.

Making Sense of It 12

1. Helpful Senses
2. five
3. ear
4. nose

Lucy and Rosita 13

1. friends
2. special
3. picture with friends at circus

Time for School 14

1. boy
2. pencils, ruler, pencil box, crayons
3. school
color backpack red and blue

Growing 15

1. Josie Grows Up
2. She was looking at pictures of herself.
Sentences: bigger, more

Home, Sweet Home 16

1. home
2. trees
3. ground
4. caves

School Workers 17

1. school
2. teachers, custodians, bus drivers, cooks
3. care

Yard Sale 18

1. Baby Things
2. Camping Equipment
3. Furniture
4. Baseball Equipment

What a Recipe! 19

1. 6
2. 1
3. 3 hours
4. cheese
5. French bread, crackers
6. six

Picture Perfect 20

Postcard should show the scene described by Mark in his note.

Where's Sassy? **21**

1. a poster
2. a girl
Picture should show an orange, black, and white cat named Sassy.

The Morning Route **22–23**

1. morning
2. seven
3. ten
4. school
morning, seven, ten, school

Watch Out! **24**

1. Bertha Butterfly
2. on a flower
3. a kitten
4. no

Any Mail Today? **25**

1. Joey
2. four
3. one
4. two
Joey, four, one, two

Piñatas **26**

1. c. a piñata.
2. b. of paper, glue, and a pot or balloon.
3. d. like an animal.
4. a. with candy and toys.

Maria's Turn **27**

Pictures will vary. Might show blindfolded girl holding a stick after breaking the piñata. Candy and toys could be on the floor.

Tide Pool Peering **28**

1. Samantha
2. tide pool
3. fish, starfish, crabs

Look Up! **29**

1. helicopter
2. many directions
3. very useful
helicopter, many directions, very useful

A Suitable Name **30**

lizard, looks, frilled lizard, name, frilly fan

What's a Moropus? **31**

Pictures will vary. They should show an animal that resembles a horse with long front legs and claw-like feet.

Petra's Piggy Bank **32**

1. Petra
2. saving money
3. to buy a kite
4. a parrot
5. five dollars
6. yes

Platypus **33**

1. Australia
2. duckbill
3. webbed feet
4. late evening

"Bee" Strong **34**

1. Buzz Bee
2. strong
3. cat food
4. bigger
5. Buzz Bee, strong, cat food, bigger

Oops! **35**

mouse, glass door, cat, looked, scared, raced, woodpile

An Old-Time Train Ride **36–37**

1. Virginia City

2. 8:00 A.M.
3. four
4. five hours
Answers will vary but should include the city of departure, time train leaves, the stops, and length of trip.

Pete's Plant **38**

Pete planted a seed. He watered it every day. It grew into a big, yellow sunflower.

Just Fold It **39**

art, Japan, folding, sheet, paper, beautiful, useful

Dressed for the Parade **40**

Tuffy, costume, parade

Pictures will vary but should reflect the description of Tuffy in the story (dog with hat, ruffle, and a yellow balloon).

What a Change! **41**

1. Brad scooped a tadpole out of the creek.
2. The tadpole grew bigger; hind and front legs appeared; the tadpole's head changed; the gills disappeared.
3. The tadpole became a frog.

Where's Dinner? **42**

1. This story is about bats.
2. Many bats eat insects.
3. Bats use their voices and ears to find insects.
4. An echo tells a bat how far away and where an insect is moving.

A Seasonal Thing **43**

Possible underlined and copied sentences: There are four seasons. They are called winter, spring, summer, and fall. Each season is different.

Strong Winds **44**

Answers will vary. Possible answer: A hurricane is a storm that forms over an ocean. It moves to land in whirling, rainy clouds. The center is called the "eye." A tornado is a funnel-shaped storm. It swirls and touches the ground. Often tornadoes have no rain.

Shooting Stars **45**

Answers will vary. Possible answer: Meteors are rocks from far out in space that fall into the earth's atmosphere. Meteors that land on earth are called meteorites.